Souad Labbize

My Soul Has No Corners

Translated from the French by

Susanna Lang

DIÁLOGOS
DIALOGOSBOOKS.COM

My Soul Has No Corners
Souad Labbize
Translated by Susanna Lang

French original copyrights:
Brouillons Amoureux: © Editions Des Lisières, 2017
"Baluchon d'exil", in *Je franchis les barbelés*, © Éditions Bruno Doucey, 2019

The version of *Brouillons amoureux (Drafts of Love)* herein includes 14 new poems not previously published in French.

Printed in the U.S.A.

Book design: Bill Lavender
Front cover art by Annie Kurkdjian © 2022

Library of Congress Control Number: 2023938909
Labbize, Souad
with Susanna Lang (translator)
My Soul Has No Corners / Souad Labbize;
p. cm.
ISBN: 978-1-956921-17-5 (pbk.)

DIÁLOGOS
dialogosbooks.com

Mon âme n'a pas de coins
My Soul Has No Corners

Guest

for Souad Labbize

I have made myself at home
in the house of your words

One word laid on the next
thick layers of mortar
to keep out the wind

A room with no corners
couscous steams in the pot
fragrant with saffron
coriander and juniper berries

You took me to the market
that reminded you of the Maghreb
piles of gold and copper spices

This is not my home
but I would like to stay here
for a while

—*Susanna Lang*

Mon âme n'a pas de coins

My Soul Has No Corners

Brouillons amoureux

Drafts of Love

Fleur d'amandier
tu n'as pas de petit nom
qui te ressemble

Almond flower
no diminutive
fits you

Grammaire amoureuse
dans je pense à toi
je ne suis pas
le sujet de la phrase

A loving grammar
when I say *I'm thinking of you*
I am not
the subject of the sentence

En classe d'amour
je m'asseyais au fond
loin des studieuses qui préparaient
carrière familiale et sociale
enfoncée tête sur le pupitre
j'écoutais la rumeur
des chahuteuses averties
me laissais bercer
par le bien-être des assoupies

et puis j'ai quitté l'école
sans diplôme

In love class
I sat in the back
far from the girls who studied hard
for careers in family and society
resting my head on my desk
I listened to the rumble
of the know-it-all troublemakers
let myself be cradled
by the ease of the sleepers

and then I dropped out of school
without a diploma

Avant de t'appeler
pour le grand aveu
je mets de l'ordre
sur le terrain de jeu
de mon silence
les mots sages s'installent
sur le banc de remplaçants
je ne les dirai
qu'en cas de panne

Before I call you
with my full confession
I set up
the playing field
of my silence
wise words settle
on the bench
I will only speak them
in case of a breakdown

Tes mains sont un bocal
de bonbons moelleux
je suis l'enfant
derrière la vitrine

Your hands are a bowl
of sweet bonbons
I am the child
outside the shop window

Suspendue à tes lèvres
j'attends la suite
tu prépares
la matière à fumer
ta bouche qui sait faire
humecte le bord du papier
sans frôler l'herbe tassée

Suspended from your lips
I wait for what's next
you prepare
the smoking materials
your mouth knows what to do
how to dampen the edge of the paper
without touching the tamped weed

J'ai plié mon cœur
avant le rendez-vous
dans la poche étroite
de la nouvelle chemise
après le rendez-vous
j'ai fait une lessive
la chemise a rétréci
et mon cœur avec

Before we met
I folded my heart
into the narrow pocket
of a new shirt
after we met
I put my shirt in the wash
it shrank and
with it my heart

Sur l'épouvantail transi
j'ai mis l'écharpe
de l'amante revêche

I wrapped a scarf
around the frozen scarecrow
it belonged to the prickly
woman I love

Tu n'es pas venue
j'ai versé l'eau frémissante
dans le verre à pied
la fleur de thé a déployé
son amertume

You didn't come
I poured boiling water
into the wineglass
the tea bloomed
with its bitter fragrance

Une passante s'éloigne
enfonce les mains dans les poches
quand elle aura disparu
j'oublierai tes dernières paroles
je ne sais plus
si tu m'as dit
à bientôt ou adieu
ou les deux à la fois
toi tu sais si bien dire
des formules gigognes
faciles à emboîter

tu n'as peut-être rien dit
d'aussi important

A woman walks by
hands in her pockets
once she has passed out of sight
I'll forget your last words
I no longer know
if you said
later or *goodbye*
or both at once
you know so well
how to fit one phrase inside another
like nesting dolls

maybe you didn't say anything
so important

Et tu disparais de l'écran
je ne sais quel nom donner
à ce qui accroche ses ballerines
à ta fenêtre éphémère
la foule de mots debout
aux frontières de la voix
fait palpiter les coroles du soupir
puis se disperse alentour

And you vanish from the screen
what name can I give
to what hangs its ballet slippers
from your temporary window
the crowd of words that stands
at the frontiers of the voice
flutters the corollas of a sigh
then scatters all around

M'attendras-tu dans le rêve
où je te cherche à l'aube
quand le sommeil vient
se glisser entre nous

Will you wait for me in the dream
where I look for you at dawn
when sleep comes
slipping between us

Ne découpe pas
mon cœur en rondelles
je ne saurai le rassembler
dans l'ordre

Don't slice
my heart in rings
I won't know how
to set them back in place

Peu de choses
je sais sur toi
de la longueur d'un fil
à occuper un chat
je le fixe à la queue du rêve
et me laisse emporter

The little bit
I know of you
long as a string
that will entertain a cat
I tie it to the dream's tail
and let myself be carried away

J'ai de la chance
l'usine onirique
où je travaille de nuit
allongée dans mon lit
produit de l'éphémère
encore heureux
l'État ne taxe pas
les bénéfices du songe

I'm fortunate
the dream factory
where I work nights
stretched out in bed
produces the ephemeral
and thank goodness
the government doesn't tax
profits from dreams

Tu t'assois
à l'autre bout du canapé
je ne sais pas où chercher
les fragments qui manquent
au puzzle entre nous

You are sitting
at the other end of the sofa
I don't know where to search
for the missing pieces
of the puzzle between us

Ton nom vibre
enfin sur l'écran
la chatte revient
caresse la fenêtre
se frotte à la vitre
se roule sur elle-même
ses miaulements sourds
me rappellent que
je ne l'ai pas nourrie

At last your name
vibrates on the screen
the cat returns
caresses the window
rubs against the pane
rolls up in a ball
her muffled cries
remind me
I have not fed her

Ne me fixe pas
il y a dans tes yeux
le reflet indiscret
de ce qui échappe
à ma pudeur
quand tu apparais

Don't stare at me
I see in your eyes
the indiscreet image
of what escapes
my modesty
when you appear

Te voici proche
du bouton discret
angle mort
de ma géologie intime
tu fouilles mes territoires caverneux
ma peau rempart docile
à ta bouche offerte
ta langue aqueduc
achemine l'eau rare
gouttes précieuses
stalactites
illuminent la pente
vers la plaine du repos
bientôt l'une de nous
atteindra le sommet
de la via ferrata
balisée par l'autre
me voici proche
de la délivrance
ma voix agrippée
à la rampe brûlante
de l'ultime échelon

une lueur éclaire
un sol de stalagmites

Now you come near
the unobtrusive bud
blind spot
of my intimate geology
you explore my cavernous terrain
skin a rampart
undefended to the mouth you offer
your tongue an aqueduct
bringing scarce water
precious drops
stalactites
light up the slope
toward the plain of repose
soon one of us
will reach the summit
of the via ferrata
the other has blazed
now I come near
my deliverance
my voice gripping
the fiery rail
of the last step

lightning reveals
a floor of stalagmites

Humeur d'avril
le lit aurait pu deviner
qu'il resterait défait
pour des motifs incertains
nous aurions pu cueillir
entre les lignes de l'agenda
le temps d'un frôlement

An April mood
the bed could have guessed
it would remain unmade
for no particular reason
in between agenda items
we could have stolen
a moment's caress

Tes mains j'ai attendu
qu'elles disent
quelque chose à ma main
elles n'ont rien vu
la chaleur de tes poches
les aveuglait

I waited for your hands
to say something
to my hand
they saw nothing
your warm pockets
blinded them

Suffirait qu'elle
tâte mon pouls
quand ses cils balaient
la poussière accumulée
sur le seuil de mon cœur

It would be enough
for her to feel my pulse
when her lashes sweep
the dust gathered
on the doorstep of my heart

Tu venais jouer
au jeu du oui et non
je jouais au docteur
tu n'étais pas malade
tu étais gardienne de but
j'étais dans ton équipe
quand j'approchais
de la surface de réparation
tes mains en triangle
me barraient le passage

You came to play
the game of yes and no
I was playing doctor
you weren't sick
you were goalkeeper
I was on your team
when I came near
the penalty box
your hands formed a triangle
blocking my way

Je prends par la main
les mots que tu ne dis pas
les emmener en balade
leur ferait du bien
les mots enfermés
aiment sortir avec les autres
qu'ils regardent jouer
à travers la vitre
je prends par l'autre main
mes petits mots assis
sur le tourniquet qui grince
tes mots et les miens
se regardent derrière mon dos
si j'avais des chaussures à lacets
je m'agenouillerais pour les nouer
tes mots et les miens
en profiteraient pour courir ensemble
vers la clairière des fusillés
et je laisserais faire
en ne pensant à rien

I take your unspoken
words by the hand
it would do them good
to go out for a walk
cooped up inside
words long to join others
they can see playing
through the window
in the other hand I take
my own little words
sitting on the squeaky merry-go-round
your words and mine
look at each other behind my back
if my shoes had laces
I'd kneel down to tie them
your words and mine
would run off together
toward the clearing where
the heroes were shot
I'd let them run
and think nothing of it

Dans un monde parfait
les doigts d'une seule main
devraient suffire à compter
les jours sans tendresse

In a perfect world
the fingers of one hand
should be enough to count
the days without tenderness

Grosse faim en pensant
au goût de l'amour perdu
j'ai mis à chauffer
le reste de soupe
aux légumes de mai
j'avais la flemme
de préparer un couscous
la pluie taquinait les plantes
derrière la buée de la vitre
je pensais à tous les retards
le tien
le printemps
l'amour
les légumes de printemps
la pluie n'a pas fait attention
au désordre de mes pensées
quand la buée s'est épaissie
je me suis souvenue
de ma grosse faim

I was so hungry
thinking how love used to taste
I turned on the stove
to warm the leftover soup
made with spring vegetables
I didn't have the energy
to make a couscous
rain teased the plants
outside the foggy window
I thought of all that's been delayed
you
spring
love
spring vegetables
the rain paid no attention
to my chaotic thoughts
when the fog thickened
I remembered
my great hunger

Tes baisers raccommodent
ma bouche entrouverte
sur l'indicible
ton amour est un atelier
de cordonnier occupé
j'y vais sans illusion
sur la date de réparation

Your kisses repair
my mouth half open
to what can't be said
your love is the shop
of a busy cobbler
I go there with no illusions
about when the work will be done

Tandis que j'essaie de te dire
je ne sais quoi de sérieux
un huit s'allonge sur ta bouche
il vient souvent écouter
ce que j'ai à te dire
et creuse le dos
sur le sofa de tes lèvres

While I try to make
some kind of serious comment
a figure eight reclines on your mouth
it often comes to hear
what I say to you
and arches its back
on the sofa of your lips

Croquer une pomme je
ne pense pas à Adam le
goût de ta bouche si tu
croquais un bout de la
pomme Ève ne pensait
pas à Adam le goût d'une
bouche de qui pouvait–
elle rêver sinon de Lilith

Biting into an apple I do
not think about Adam
the taste of your mouth
if you bit into the apple
Eve wasn't thinking
about Adam the taste
of a mouth who could
she dream of but Lilith

Le panier à linge
attend le retour des draps
tendus sur la corde
le soleil la brise de juin
ont effacé l'effluve
de l'amante imaginaire
demain j'irai chercher
une lessive qui rappelle
l'alchimie de nos corps

The laundry basket
waits for the sheets
hung on the line
sun the June breeze
have erased the scent
of the imaginary lover
tomorrow I will look for
a soap that recalls
the alchemy of our bodies

Ton rejet
je le retourne
entre mes doigts
pièce de monnaie
qui ne sert qu'à
compléter une somme
le prix d'un paquet
de mouchoirs doux

Your rejection
I worry it like beads
between my fingers
a coin
good for nothing
but to make up a sum
the price of a pack
of soft tissues

Le bonheur attendu
n'a rendez-vous avec
personne ici
personne là-bas
que fait-il seul
quand il rentre le soir
dans une chambre vide

Anticipated joy
has no rendezvous with
anyone here
anyone there
what does it do in the evening
returning alone
to an empty room

À l'heure où les corps se déplient
j'achemine vers ton chevet
un rêve que tu décoifferas
pendant que je le préparais
il trépignait d'impatience
je n'ai pas eu le temps
de tout lui dire
il te dira la moitié des choses
pendant que tu lui passeras
la main dans les cheveux

When it's time for our bodies to stretch out
I send a dream to your bedside
where you will ruffle its curls
while I got the dream ready
it stamped impatiently
I didn't have time
to say everything
it will tell you half of what I meant
while you run your hand
through its hair

Comme une première fois
tu te réveilleras près de moi
tu auras une réponse
qui nécessite une question

As if for the first time
you will wake up beside me
you will have an answer
that demands a question

Je ne sais que faire
des raisons de t'aimer
une saison précoce
commence et finit
au milieu d'une autre
sans même nous faire
changer de vêtements

I don't know what to make
of the reasons to love you
an early season
begins and ends
in the midst of another
we don't even have to
change our clothes

Au parloir de mon poignet
le temps s'arrête
sous la vitre du cadran
l'étreinte des aiguilles
de ma vieille montre
dure soixante secondes
une minute
s'embrasser
douter
se séparer

In the parlor
I wear on my arm
time stands still
under the crystal
the hands of my old watch embrace
for sixty seconds
one minute
to kiss
doubt
part

L'écheveau de tes lieux
traverse mes bazars
tu déménages à ta guise
sans laisser d'adresse
fermant échoppe
ouvrant boutique
un soir de lune

The net of your premises
spans my bazaars
you change locations when you like
without leaving an address
close one stall
open another shop
in one moonlit evening

J'ai pisté tes traces
quelques indices
sur la neige d'une nuit
le désir courait plus vite
que mes jambes
mon haleine fiévreuse
faisait fondre
l'empreinte de tes pas

I followed your tracks
a few signs
on the snow fallen overnight
desire ran faster
than my legs
my feverish breath
melted the traces
of your steps

Tu poses les mains
à plat
je croise les pieds
sous la table
ainsi débute
une conversation grave
le fil à plomb
tendu par tes lèvres
s'écrase sur mes pieds

You place your hands
flat
I cross my ankles
under the table
so begins
a weighty conversation
the plumb line
dropped from your lips
crashes into my feet

Tes paroles d'un soir
portent un pyjama
de petit garçon
je les borde
les accompagne
jusqu'à l'invisible lisière
j'éteins la lumière
et ferme la porte

le matin d'ici
les trouve dans mon lit
comme l'enfant venu
se blottir au point du jour

Your words from that night
wear pajamas
like a little boy
I tuck them in
go with them
as far as the invisible border
turn out the light
and close the door

here, morning
finds them in my bed
like the child
come to snuggle at dawn

Te dire quoi
si les mots n'ont plus
de dents pour mordiller
le lobe de ton oreille

What can I tell you
if words no longer
have teeth to nibble
the lobe of your ear

Brouillon froissé d'un poème
l'amante blottie
au bord d'une rime
s'étire
déroule le dos
déplie les jambes
rampe entre les plis

Crumpled draft of a poem
the lover curled
at the edge of a rhyme
she stretches
unwinds her spine
unfolds her legs
crawls between the creases

Baluchon d'exil

Bindle of Exile

I

Dans le mot exil
il y a une paire de semelles
qui ne se parlent plus
un baluchon plié
en haut du placard
une boussole rongée de remords
un dictionnaire bilingue
qui dit peu de choses
de l'exil
juste assez
pour cacher sa douleur

des semelles
un baluchon
une boussole
qui ne rentrent pas
dans la traduction
du mot exil

une boussole
des semelles
un baluchon
qui ne rêvent plus
du droit au retour

I

In the word exile
a pair of soles
that no longer speak to each other
a bindle folded away
on the top shelf of a closet
a compass rusty with remorse
a bilingual dictionary
that doesn't say much
about exile
just enough
to hide its pain

two soles
a bindle
a compass
that do not enter
into the translation
of the word exile

a compass
two soles
a bindle
that no longer dream
of the right of return

2

Tu n'es pas venue
comme prévu

alors l'attente
s'est mise à chuchoter
les dialectes de l'ennui

nous n'avions rien
à t'offrir
pas de fleurs
pour t'accueillir
nos mains brandissaient
des bouquets invisibles
cueillis délicatement
dans le champ en jachère
au repos dans le rêve

nous avons parlé de toi
à la buée déposée par le cri
à la levure qui manque au pain
à la page arrachée au passeport
à l'empreinte de la gifle
nos paroles dépassaient nos pensées
des fleurs d'amandier
sont apparues

2

You did not arrive
as arranged

and so the wait
began to whisper
in the dialects of boredom

we had nothing
to offer you
no flowers
to welcome you
our hands brandished
invisible bouquets
flowers gathered with care
from the fallow field
resting in dreams

we spoke of you
to the fog left behind by our cries
to the yeast left out of the bread
to the page torn out of the passport
to the mark left by a slap across the face
our words ran ahead of our thoughts
almond flowers
appeared

dans nos bouquets invisibles
et le champ en sommeil dit
le temps est venu
de cultiver la parcelle en lisière
mais tu n'es pas venue

tu n'es pas venue
comme prévu

in our invisible bouquets
and the sleeping field said
the time has come
to plant that acre of land at the edge
but you didn't arrive

you did not arrive
as arranged

3

Mon âme n'a pas
de coins
quand j'y reviens
les bras chargés
d'un nouveau chagrin
je ne trouve nulle part
ce qui peut ressembler
à un coin de table
où prendre un goûter
à côté d'une paire de mains
qui écossent des petits pois
mon âme je ne sais pas
qui l'a conçue
un architecte qui croit
aux vertus circulaires
des maisons d'âmes
où il n'y a pas de place
pour un seul coin

3

My soul has no
corners
when I return
with an armload
of new grief
I can't find
anything like
the corner of a table
where I could have a snack
next to a pair of hands
shelling peas
I don't know
who conceived my soul
an architect who believes
in the circular virtues
of soul houses
without room
for a single corner

4

J'ai frotté mes semelles
l'une contre l'autre
secoué mon accent
pané ma langue
j'ai fait ce qu'il fallait
pour quitter incognito
pourtant il me retrouve
le matin je ne sais dire
si c'est un cauchemar
ou juste un rêve anodin
qu'on ne raconte à personne
il y'a pas de nom
pour ce qui n'est
ni doux rêve
ni cauchemar
et qui m'attend la nuit
sans décliner son identité
que je reconnais
sans pouvoir nommer

4

I scrubbed my soles
against each other
shook out my accent
coated my tongue
did everything I could
to depart incognito
still it finds me
come morning I can't say
if it was a nightmare
or just a harmless dream
you wouldn't mention to anyone
there is no word
for what is neither
a sweet dream
nor a nightmare
for what waits for me each night
without identifying itself
I recognize it
but can't give it a name

5

À force d'y croire
comme une imbécile
j'irai à l'école
un dimanche matin
avec la moitié de la classe
je plierai ma voix en quatre
enveloppe gris-bleu
en papier recyclé
épais comme un linceul
qui a déjà servi
la fente aura la taille
d'une bouche figée
qui ne sait pas embrasser
comme un jour de long voyage
peur de rater le train
me tromper de locomotive
monter dans le wagon aveugle
qui connaît le chemin
du souvenir abject

5

Believing in it
like an idiot
I'll go to school
on a Sunday morning
with half the class
fold my voice in quarters
blue-grey envelope
of recycled paper
thick as a shroud
that's been used before
the slot shaped like
a mouth so stiff
it doesn't know how to kiss
like a long day of travel
afraid I'll miss the train
or take the wrong one
climb into the cattle car
that knows the route
taken by abject memory

6

Qui
nous remerciera
nous
peuple de parias
d'avoir tu nos peines
et dans un coffre d'aéroport
plié nos langues exubérantes
l'adresse d'un cimetière
pour le voyage du retour

Qui

6

Who
will thank us
we
an outcast people
who hushed our griefs
and in an airport locker
stored our ardent languages
the address of a cemetery
for the return trip

Who

7

Ne comptez pas
sur mon petit balcon
par ce temps humide
la lessive d'une semaine
tarde à sécher
il n'y a pas de place
pour un autre drap
fût-il tricolore
je ne sais quel savon
ferait l'affaire
laver les vieux drapeaux
est affaire de lavandières
veuves de soldats inconnus
celles que je connais
sont mortes de chagrin
sur une planche à laver

7

Don't count on
my small balcony
in this humid weather
the week's wash
dries slowly
there's no room
for another sheet
even tricolor
I don't know what soap
could do the job
washing old flags
is a job for washerwomen
widows of unknown soldiers
the ones I know
died of heartbreak
over a washboard

8

Dans le hall de l'immeuble
une boîte anonyme
porte une étiquette
inconnue a cette adresse

8

In the apartment lobby
a mailbox
with a note
Address unknown

9

Les gens riches
garent leurs rêves d'enfant
dans des garages proprets
pour les protéger
de l'oxydation
mes rêves d'enfant
couchent dehors
sur le bitume qui renifle
les semelles de voyageurs
ils ne craignent pas
la rouille qui couvre leur carcasse
d'un hâle de marin
mes rêves d'enfant ont grandi
dans les rues encombrées
de songes vagabonds
qu'un rien nourrit
quand ils me manquent
je sais où les trouver

9

The rich
park their childhood dreams
in nice clean garages
to protect them
from oxidation
my childhood dreams
sleep outside
on asphalt that sniffs
at the soles of strangers
my dreams are not afraid
of the rust that covers their bones
like a sailor's weathered skin
my childhood dreams grew up
on streets crowded
with wandering fantasies
living on almost nothing
when I miss them
I know where to find them

10

Je demande au Sahara
ce qu'il attend
il me répond
d'un air entendu
je suis butin
du sablier cosmique

10

I ask the Sahara
what it is waiting for
the desert answers
with a knowing air
I was stolen
from the cosmic hourglass

II

Jouer à pile
exil
face
terre natale
marcher
pieds joints
sur le listel
ligne d'horizon striée
entre ici
et là-bas

II

If it's tails
exile
heads
native soil
walk
with both feet
on the coin's curved edge
striated horizon
between here
and over there

12

Là où le Ciel
ne me voit
qu'à moitié
deux alphabets tissent
refuge éphémère
qui ne ressemble
pas au paradis
pas à l'enfer

le problème des alphabets
est d'ordre mathématique
ensembles fermés
qui tournent en rond
en attendant que les voisins
les invitent à une joute
ou une auberge espagnole

12

Where Heaven
only sees
half of me
two alphabets weave
a temporary shelter
that's not like
paradise
not like hell

the problem with alphabets
is mathematical
closed sets
that turn in circles
waiting for the neighbors'
invitation to a joust
or a potluck supper

13

J'apprends à transformer
le silence en preuves
paroles abruties
par une garde à vue
dans les replis de la gorge

13

I learn to transform
silence into evidence
words stupefied
by their detention
in the recesses of the throat

14

Te décrire l'exil
me planter à l'envers
tête en bas
jambes en équilibre
les larmes croient arroser
les nouvelles racines

14

To show you exile
I turn myself upside down
head below
legs balanced in air
my tears think they're watering
new roots

15

Je n'aime vraiment pas
les pages sans marges
longues comme une année
sans vacances
mais les pages quadrillées
arriver essoufflée au bout
d'une ligne besogneuse
m'échouer à l'est du paragraphe
et puis et puis
esquisser felouque
bleue pavillon blanc
traverser le texte
chargée de saisons
Les rames se partagent
l'alphabet maternel
en consonnes voyelles
pour atteindre l'ouest
en penchant du côté
des consonnes rares
et puis et puis
reprendre la fable
de l'encre qui attend
de s'évaporer
elle aussi veut vivre
loin du flocon joli

15

I really don't like
pages without margins
long as a year
without vacations
graph paper is best
I gasp for breath
at the end of an overworked line
run aground east of the paragraph
and then and then
sketch a small boat
blue with a white flag
sail across the text
to the western shore
with a cargo of seasons
The oars divide
my first alphabet
into consonants and vowels
leaning into
the rarest consonants
and then and then
I turn back to the fable
of the ink
waiting to evaporate
the ink wants to live too
far from the pretty bottle

la page à nourrir
est une île
la mienne s'écrit
de gauche à droite
et puis et puis
s'abreuve le moment venu
sur la rive est où j'ai posé
l'encrier malgré moi

the page I feed
is an island
mine is written
left to right
and then and then
at the right moment it takes a drink
on the east bank where I set
the inkwell despite myself

Il manque à ma langue
ces mots charnus
fragiles de ne pas exister
ils errent pieds nus
les ronces les griffent
quand ils tentent de fuir
le sous-bois d'un cauchemar
Ils se faufilent le matin
près de syllabes inconsolables
de n'avoir pas servi
à habiller un signifié
mots indispensables
qui pourraient exister
dire l'instant
où j'émerge d'un rêve
nommer la tentative d'y revenir
intercepter un vœu
accroché à un regard
le reconnaître
il manque aux poètes
ces mots que je poursuis
avec un outil inconnu
qui n'a pas de nom
lui non plus

16

My language just doesn't have
those plump words
weakened by not existing
they wander barefoot
scratched by brambles
when they try to escape
the undergrowth of a nightmare
Mornings they sidle up
to disconsolate syllables
that have not served
to clothe a meaning
indispensable words
that could exist
could speak the moment
when I emerge from a dream
could name my effort to recover it
intercept the desire
clinging to a glance
could recognize it
poets just don't have
these words that I pursue
with an unfamiliar tool
that also lacks
a name

17

L'histoire
pour border l'enfant
raconte-la-moi
les matins incertains

17

That story
for tucking a child into bed
tell it to me
on uncertain mornings

18

Va et viens
balançoire
ne gémis pas
ne ralentis pas
ne t'emballe pas
que je ne sache pas
si je suis poussée
ou celle qui pousse

18

Go and come back
swing
don't cry
don't slow down
don't get carried away
so I won't know
if I'm the one being pushed
or the one who pushes

19

La géostratégie de l'exil
se couche tôt
j'en profite pour ranger
mon désordre intime
les choses reviennent
à leur place ordinaire
mer au nord
désert au sud
figuier barbare
en guise d'horizon

19

The geostrategy of exile
goes to bed early
a good opportunity
to pick up my private mess
everything goes back
where it belongs
the sea to the north
desert to the south
prickly pear cactus
in lieu of a horizon

20

Il arrive que le seuil
d'une demeure inconnue
donne une sensation furtive
de déjà-vu
on croit arriver
à l'endroit où l'on manque

20

Sometimes the entrance
to an unfamiliar house
gives you a fleeting sense
of déjà vu
as if you've found
the place where you've been missing

21

Ma voisine d'Alger
n'avait pas de lave-linge
mais le goût
des batailles navales
face à la poussière de l'Histoire
elle reprenait les négociations
contre les ennemis
de la nation et les autres
elle savait comment
laver le linge souillé
jambes écartées
autour d'une bassine
elle laissait tremper
les discours résistants
du président à vie
de l'imam officiel
parfois de Dieu lui-même
au moment de frotter
elle injuriait
c'était sa façon
de faire de la politique

21

My neighbor in Algiers
didn't have a washer
but she did have a taste
for naval battles
confronting the dust of History
she resumed negotiations
against the enemies
of the nation and everyone else
she knew how to
wash dirty laundry
legs straddling
a washtub
she soaked
the stubborn tirades
of the President for Life
the official imam
sometimes God himself
she cursed
as she scrubbed
it was her way
to be political

22

Dans ma bouche maternelle
le mot guerre est court
celle qui l'a inventé
n'a pas eu le temps
de le finir
harb commence par une douleur
au fond de la gorge
et meurt en atteignant
le bout des lèvres

22

In my mother tongue
the word for war is short
the woman who invented it
didn't have time
to finish the work
harb begins with pain
in the back of your throat
and dies when it reaches
your lips

23

Le troisième jour
pour remplir ma gourde
j'ai percé les ampoules
de mes pieds
lapé l'encre
du passeport
mâché le papier officiel
les initiales de mon nom
se sont imprimées sur mes lèvres

le septième jour
j'ai chaussé mon euphorie
survolé la dernière dune
vers la rive nord du mirage

le quarantième jour
je me suis présentée
à la cérémonie des diplômes
le désert m'a remis
une attestation honorifique

je me suis assise
sur un amoncellement d'os
j'ai attendu le passeur

23

On the third day
I lanced the blisters
on my feet
to fill my canteen
lapped up the ink
on my passport
chewed the official paper
my initials
stamped on my lips

on the seventh day
I put shoes on my euphoria
flew over the last dune
toward the north shore of the mirage

on the fortieth day
I presented myself
at the graduation ceremony
the desert awarded me
an honorary degree

I sat down
on a pile of bones
to wait for the trafficker

24

Si je pouvais
retrouver un peu de ma foi
croire à un miracle
murmurer une prière
à mon ex-dieu
dans une langue intime
puis revenir à ma place
devant l'écran
attendre la nouvelle
du cessez-le-feu

24

If I could
regain a little faith
believe in a miracle
murmur a prayer
in a private language
to my ex-god
then return to my seat
in front of the screen
wait for news
of the cease-fire

25

Parfois
un seul signe de ponctuation
me sépare de toi

une faucille
qui ne sait pas
ce qu'elle fait
si loin du champ
ni comment
elle en est arrivée
à un boulot de vigile

parfois
ce signe prend
la forme d'un rond-point
au bout d'une impasse
une interrogation de plus
qui n'aura pas de réponse
(ni de toi ni de moi)

un point d'interrogation
a l'utilité d'un cintre
quand un petit crochet
suffit à suspendre

25

Sometimes
a single punctuation mark
comes between us

a sickle
that doesn't know
what it's doing
so far from the field
nor how
it landed in this job
as a night watchman

sometimes
this mark takes the form
of a traffic circle
at the end of a cul-de-sac
one more interrogation
that won't lead to an answer
(from you or me)

a question mark
is useful as a hanger
when a small hook
meets your need

26

Nous commencions à peine
le jeu de la rébellion
ils nous ont cueillis
d'une branche haute
du jardin de l'ogre
l'un de nous avait oublié
de fermer la porte
nos jouets de guerre
étaient éparpillés
au pied de nos cris
l'appel des mères
suppliait l'écho
de nous prévenir
l'écho s'était heurté
aux boucliers transparents
nous connaissions mieux qu'eux
les règles de nos jeux
méchants contre gentils
cow-boys contre Indiens
nous échangions nos rôles
par souci d'équité
nous étions en même temps
les gentils et les méchants
nous nous redressions
après chaque bataille

26

We had just started
the game of rebellion
they plucked us
from a high branch
in the ogre's garden
one of us had forgotten
to close the gate
our war toys
scattered
beneath our shrieks
our mothers called
begging the echo
to warn us
the echo hurtled
into transparent shields
we knew the rules of the game
better than they did
bad guys versus good guys
cowboys versus Indians
we switched roles
to be fair
good guys and bad guys
at the same time
we stood back up
after each battle

sans savoir qui de nous
avait perdu
quand ils sont venus
les cow-boys et les méchants
nous avons cru
qu'ils voulaient se joindre
à nos jeux confus

without knowing
who'd lost
when they arrived
the cowboys and bad guys
we thought
they wanted to join
our mixed-up games

27

Toi Cosette moi Gavroche
aux jeux de récréation
les Misérables c'était nous
en classe de français
nous ânonnions ton nom
Liberté
sur le cahier d'écolière
hum
ni Hugo ni Éluard
n'ont écrit un seul mot
pour nous autres
poussière de colonisées

27

You Cosette me Gavroche
at recess
we were *Les Misérables*
during French class
we recited your name
Liberté
over our schoolgirl notebooks
hmm
neither Hugo nor Éluard
wrote a single word
for us the others
the dust the colonized

28

Pour Assia Djebar

Femme qui laboures
parcelle de langue
en travers de nos gorges
j'arrive comme toi
sur un champ de douilles
crachées de part et d'autre
d'une ligne fictive
le sillon que tu creuses
abrite déjà
des graines créoles
bavardes comme pies
coquines comme perdrix
loin des maquis
criblés de paroles perdues

28

For Assia Djebar

Woman you cultivate
an acre of tongue
stretched across our throats
I come as you do
to a field of cartridges
spit from both sides
of an imaginary line
the furrow you plow
already shelters
creole seeds
gossipy as magpies
flirty as partridges
far from the maquis
riddled with lost words

29

Des molosses venus en meute
du champ de l'ennemi
ont rogné la queue du chiot
gardien de nos ruines
saura-t-il nous accueillir
quand l'exil sera fatigué
de nos va-et-vient

29

A pack of hounds
came from the enemy's field
chewed off the puppy's tail
as it stood guard over our ruins
will it still welcome us
when exile has grown tired
of our comings and goings

30

À sa machine de tissage
l'ouvrière demande
des nouvelles d'Ulysse

30

The workingwoman
asks her loom
for news of Ulysses

Pour t'embrasser sans tendresse
je n'ai pas usé mes semelles
j'ai pris l'avion et le train
vers des villes transparentes
qui ne parlent pas tes langues natales
l'accent du douanier est un parchemin
chez l'amie retrouvée
loin de toi
tes guerres
tes lamentations
la mémoire barbote
dans une cocotte
coriandre persil jouent
aux hôtesses affables
la fumée du pain
se fraie un passage
vers les portraits bicolores
d'ancêtres sérieux
d'enfants nés au pays
pendant l'absence
sur la croûte craquelée
les graines de nigelle
forment constellation
la vapeur du couscous
répand buée sur vitres

31

Traveling to our untender kiss
I did not wear out my soles
I took a plane and a train
to reach transparent cities
that do not speak your native tongues
the custom officer's accent is unfamiliar
my long lost friend lives
far from you
from your wars
your laments
memory simmers
in a pot
coriander and parsley
act as gracious hostesses
steam from the bread
makes its way
to the two-toned portraits
of grave ancestors
of children born at home
while we were gone
cumin seeds
form a constellation
on the crusty bread
vapor from the couscous
fogs the windows

la neige pour m'accueillir
se transforme en chaux
sur les façades de Montréal

snow becomes limewash
on Montreal's façades
to welcome me

32

Un bruit de porte
interrompt la rêverie
quelque chose
en profite pour filer
par l'entrebâillement
peut-être l'apaisement

32

The sound of a door
interrupts my revery
something
takes the opportunity
to slip out through the opening
it might be serenity

33

Il s'agit
de quitter le pays
légère
valise en soute
sac en cabine
le reste
n'est pas déclaré
le reste
n'a pas de bagage
à sa taille
l'avion décolle
les bagages intimes
tombent en pluie
de leur cachette

33

It's a question of
how to leave the country
lightweight
suitcase checked
bag in the overhead bin
the rest
can't be declared
the rest
can't fit
into any suitcase
the plane takes off
your private baggage
falls like rain
from its hiding place

34

Je suis la frontière
dès lors que je franchis
les barbelés
sans projet de retour

j'ouvre la porte
au garde-frontière
il passe vérifier
l'avancement des travaux
de la maquette réplique
à l'entrée du souvenir
nous discutons volume
l'échelle choisie
ne lui convient pas

34

I am the border
as soon as I clear
the barbed wire
with no plans to return

I open the door
for the border guard
he's come to check
on the construction
of a model replica
at the entrance to memory
we talk about size
he doesn't think
the scale is right

35

Je peux vous dire
le jour du couscous
nous rassemblait tous
dans des temples gourmands

les graines de semoule
se faisaient masser
entre les paumes des prêtresses
assises en cercle
autour de plats en zinc
sur des tabourets de crèche
Allah suivait avec nous
le mouvement des doigts
nous L'entendions saliver

quand la vapeur atteignait
le minaret du vendredi
nos cuillères accouraient
nous répondions en chœur
à l'appel parfumé
des couscoussiers brûlants

35

Let me tell you
the day we had couscous
gathered us all
in the temples of gluttony

the semolina
came together
in the priestesses' hands
sitting on children's stools
arranged in a circle
around zinc platters
Allah followed their gestures
as we did
we could hear Him salivate

when the steam
reached Friday's minaret
our spoons rushed in
we answered in chorus
the sweet-smelling call
of the scalding couscous pots

36

J'ai actualisé
la liste des peurs
qui transforment mon dos
en arc tendu

peur
les dimanches de match
les vendredis de prière
les lundis de retour à l'usine
avant le lever du soleil

peur
du calendrier de la foule
qui n'a pas peur
du vendredi de prière
du dimanche de match
du lundi de retour à l'usine
avant le lever du soleil

la liste de mes peurs
est une amulette
collée sur le calendrier

36

I updated
the list of fears
that transform my back
into a drawn bow

fear
of Sunday soccer matches
Friday prayers
Mondays back at the factory
before the break of day

fear
of the calendar of the crowd
that has no fear
of Friday prayers
Sunday soccer matches
Mondays back at the factory
before the break of day

the list of my fears
is an amulet
hung from the calendar

37

Tu reviens
sur les lieux
de l'épouvante
l'absence t'interroge
de quel futur proche
viens-tu
toi l'étrangère
du passé proche
je n'ai pas réussi
à atteindre l'avenir

37

You come back
to the sites
of terror
absence interrogates you
from what near future
have you arrived
you the stranger
from the recent past
I have not yet
reached the time to come

38

Qu'arrive-t-il aux paroles
qu'on ne prononce pas
rouillent-elles
sous la langue

38

What happens to the words
no one speaks
do they rust
under our tongues

39

M'endormir ailleurs
que dans mon lit
bercée par le bruissement
d'une conversation
laissez-moi sur la banquette
avec mes chaussures
qu'une main me couvre
d'une étoffe qui servira
de tapis volant

39

To fall asleep somewhere
other than my bed
lulled by the thrum
of a conversation
let me stay on the bench
with my shoes on
let a hand cover me
with a blanket that will serve
as a flying carpet

40

Nuit verticale personne
ne vient allumer
sous la cafetière
ne vient ouvrir
les persiennes
personne pour dire
réveille-toi
va chercher le pain

40

Vertical night no one
comes to turn on
the coffee
no one opens
the blinds
no one tells me
wake up
go get the bread

41

Savoir trouver
arguments
promettre au retour
qu'on y va
bientôt

41

Make a strong
case
promise on our return
we'll go back
soon

42

Mes écrits pour toi muent
en photos sépia
des fêtes après jeûne
est-ce bien moi serrée
dans des coutures d'apparat
vêtue de laine en août
en prévision de la rentrée
est-ce bien toi qui boudes
dans le murmure des lignes

42

What I've written for you
turns sepia like old photos
feasts after fasting
is that really me corseted
into formal dress
wearing wool in August
to get ready for fall
is that really you sulking
in my murmured lines

43

Entends-tu ce badaboum
c'est le cœur du tyran
encerclé à Khartoum

43

Do you hear that kaboom
it's the heart of the tyrant
besieged at Khartoum

44

Nous redoutions le vacarme
qui s'ensuivrait
il est tombé du trône
sans que nul n'entende
le bruit de la chute
étouffé par nos hourras

44

We dreaded the tumult
that would follow
he fell from the throne
but no one heard
the sound of his fall
stifled by our hurrahs

45

C'est l'alphabet de la douleur
qui t'initie aux peines récidivistes

C'est l'ancêtre tatoueuse qui te poursuit
avec l'invisible dermographe
elle te retrouvera blottie
dans ta cachette d'outre-patrie
l'encre injectera son bleu
encore et encore
dans les galeries de l'âme

45

It's the alphabet of pain
that sentences you like a repeat offender

It's your ancestor the tattooist
who follows you with her invisible needle
she will find you nestled
in your overseas hideout
the ink will inject its bruise
again and again
into the soul's passageways

46

Il tombe sur ma page
la glaise de ton silence
j'ai beau chercher
le cadavre de tes mots
je ne vois que l'écume
avoir des mains vertes
replanter ce qui reste
de ton ultime cri
que pousse un éden
entre enclume et marteau

46

The clay of your silence
muffles my page
it's no use searching
for the cadaver of your words
I see only sea foam
I will have a green thumb
replant what remains
of your last cry
may an Eden grow
between the hammer and the anvil

47

J'ai des rêves de mailles serrées
d'un tapis noué main
qu'on oublie de secouer

47

I am the strands knotted too tightly
in a rug woven by hand
that no one has remembered to shake out

Notes

Drafts of Love

I take your unspoken: There is a clearing in a forest in Angers dedicated to the members of the French Resistance who faced the Nazi firing squad there.

Bindle of Exile

#28: Assia Djebar (1936-2015) was an Algerian novelist, film maker and feminist.

#31: Souad Labbize is speaking directly to Algeria, her homeland, as she evokes a visit to her childhood friend now living in Montreal. The snow on the façades in Montreal reminds her of the limewashed houses where she grew up.

#47: This very brief poem required a great deal of discussion between Souad and myself in order to arrive at a translation that matched her idea of the poem. Here is the draft I sent her at first:

> I dream of the close weave
> a rug knotted by hand
> that we forget to shake out.

She responded that "I am the one who feels like the tight stitches," so she didn't want the word "dream" in the English poem although it appears in the French. She wanted to be shaken as she imagined the stitches also wanted to be shaken out: "The stitches are crowded together and it's a feeling of suffocation....the feeling of being crowded in a community where I can't breathe, can't move." When I proposed the translation that appears in this edition, she worried about the word "too," which I had added. My concern was that without it, the reader would simply think that the rug was well-made (the stitches are *supposed* to be tight!) rather than a metaphor for suffocation. When I have these discussions with an author, I make as strong a case as I can for the English version that seems right to me, but I believe that the poem belongs to the poet rather than to me as translator, so I also offered to remove "too" if she felt strongly about it. At that point, she told me to use my judgment.

Acknowledgments

My warmest gratitude to Souad Labbize, who trusted me with this work and guided me through it. I am also grateful to the smart, generous translators of Third Coast Translators Collective and the American Literary Translators Association, who supported my re-entry into the world of translation. A special word of thanks to Kay Heikkinen, who collaborated with me in the initial translation of *Drafts of Love*, which in its first edition was published with a translation into Arabic, Kay's language for translation.

The original version of *Brouillons amoureux* was published by Éditions des Lisières in 2017. This version has 14 new poems that have not previously been published in French.

Baluchon d'exil was published by Éditions Bruno Doucey in 2019, as a section of *Je franchis les barbelés*.

Thanks also to the editors of these journals where some of these translations first appeared:

Columbia Journal: Don't count on; In the apartment lobby; The rich; I ask the Sahara; If it's tails; Where Heaven

Delos: The laundry basket; Your rejection; In the parlor; I followed your tracks; You place your hands; Crumbled draft

Ezra: A loving grammar; Before I call you; Your hands are a bowl

The Literary Review: A woman walks by; Will you wait for me in the dream; Don't slice; I'm fortunate; You are sitting

OOMPH! Journal: Now you come near; An April mood; I waited for your hands; I take your unspoken; Your kisses repair

Souad Labbize was born in Algeria in 1965, and lived in Germany and Tunisia before moving to Toulouse, France. She has published a novel, *J'aurais voulu être un escargot (I would have liked to be a snail,* Seguier, 2011*)* and several poetry collections, including *Brouillons amoureux (Drafts of Love,* Éditions des Lisières, 2017) and more recently *Je franchis les barbelés, (Climbing Over Barbed Wire,* Éditions Bruno Doucey, 2019). The Centre Méditerranéen de Littérature honored this last publication with the 2020 Prix de la Méditerranée de la Poésie. In 2021, she released *Glisser nue sur la rampe du temps* (Envers) and *Enfiler la chemise de l'aïeule* (HETRAIE). Very committed to the cause of equality between genders, she writes in the name of all women who choose exile in order to affirm their independence.

Susanna Lang's translations of poetry include *Words in Stone* by Yves Bonnefoy (University of Massachusetts Press, 1976) and *Baalbek* by Nohad Salameh (L'Atelier du Grand Tétras, 2021). Her translations of these and other French poets are published or forthcoming in *Asymptote, Delos, Tupelo Quarterly, The Literary Review, Transference, Columbia Journal, Ezra* and *OOMPH! Journal*. Her chapbook of original poems, *Like This,* was released in 2023 by Unsolicited Press, and her third full-length collection, *Travel Notes from the River Styx*, was published by Terrapin Books in 2017. *Among Other Stones: Conversations with Yves Bonnefoy,* an e-chapbook of original poems and translations, was published by Mudlark in summer 2021. More information available at www.susannalang.com.

DIÁLOGOS
DIALOGOSBOOKS.COM

www.ingramcontent.com/pod-product-compliance
Lightning Source LLC
Chambersburg PA
CBHW021400090426
42742CB00009B/934